BUTTERFLIES

Coloring Book for Adults

By Sachin Sachdeva

ISBN: 978-1983674839

Copyright 2020, Sachin Sachdeva

This book belongs to

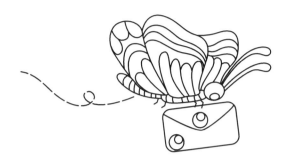

Butterflies are the most beautiful winged insects around us. In this book, you'll find whimsical butterflies decorated around flowers and also discover more wonderful things along the way. It's inspired from nature and let you explore the diversity in each coloring page.

Each coloring page is unique & handmade, illustrated in vector. I hope you enjoy coloring the pages. You can share your colored pages with me @sachdev.art on instagram and also post your artwork on my facebook group "Books by Sachin Sachdeva".

Best,
Sachin Sachdeva
Author & Illustrator

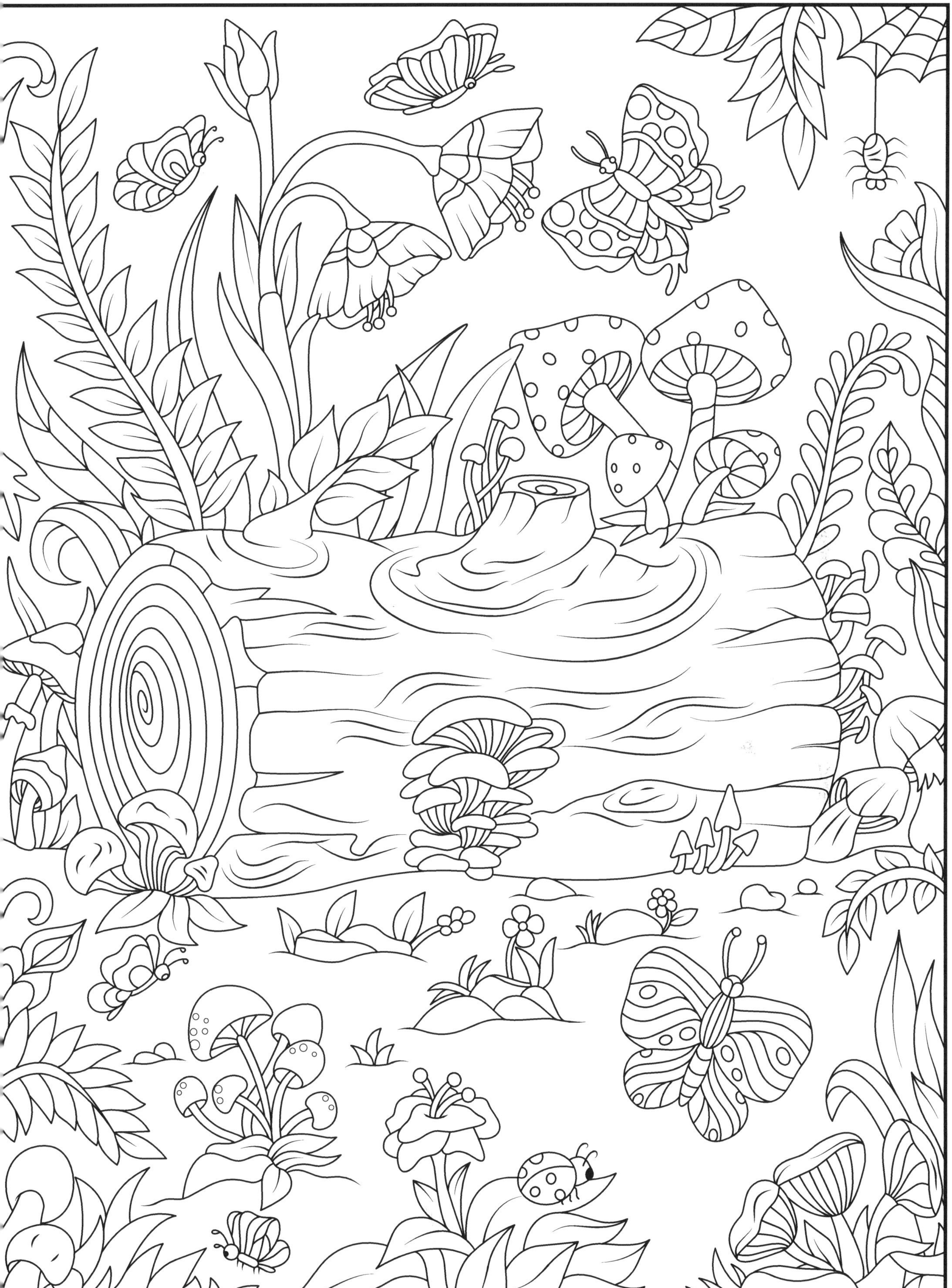

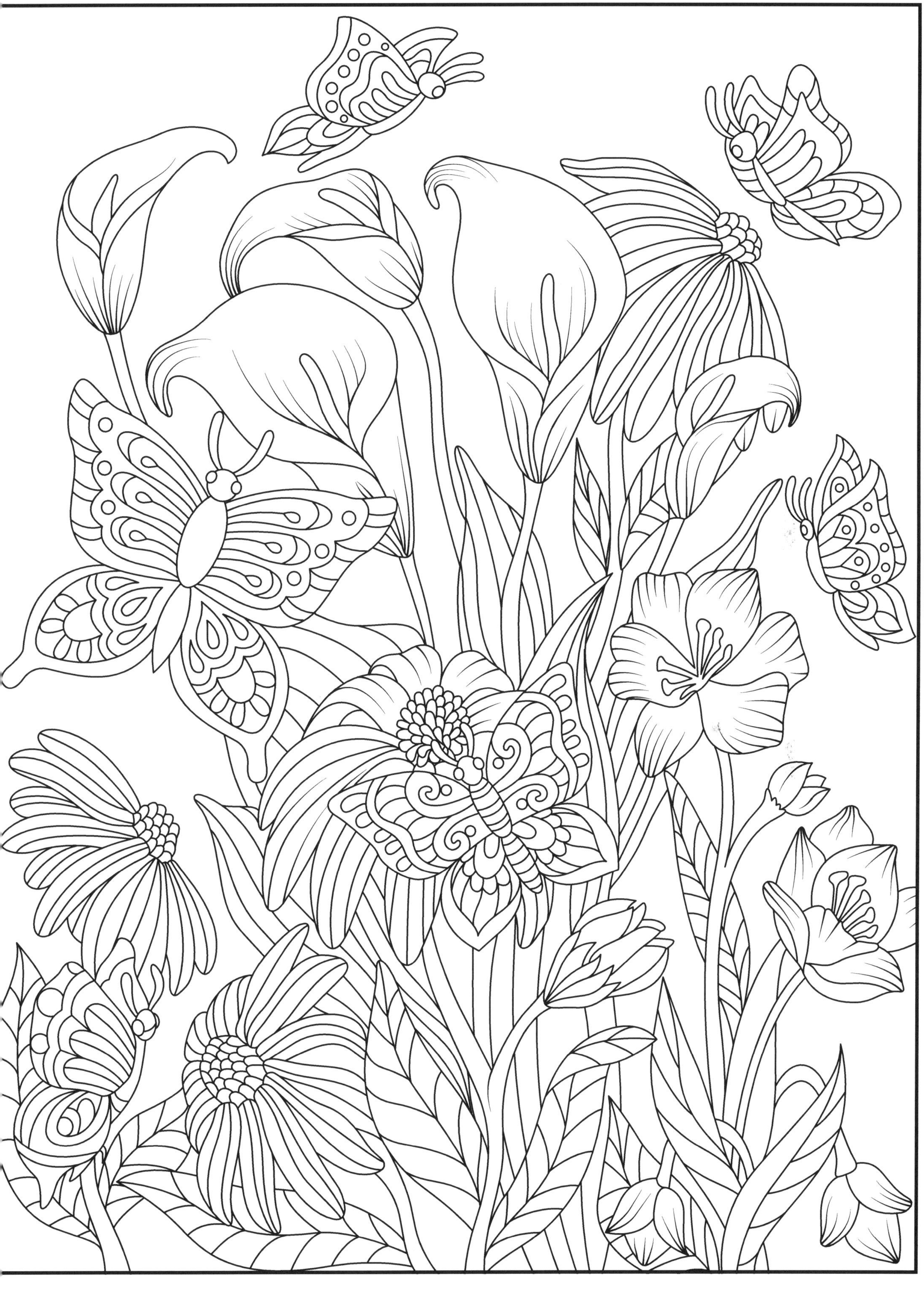

You might also like these coloring books

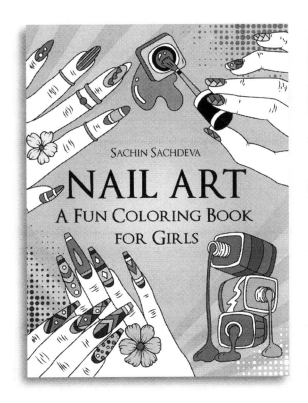

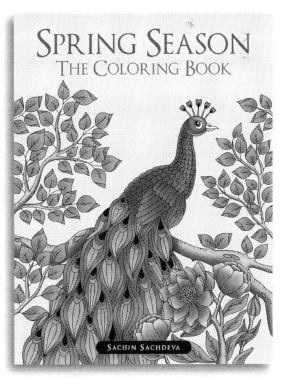

Thank you for purchasing the book. I hope you and your family members enjoyed coloring the pages.

Being a self-published author and illustrator, it's very difficult to reach out to people or spend lots of money on paid marketing. My sales rely on buyers feedback and their satisfaction which motivates me to create more quality content for people of all ages especially children.

Kindly **leave ratings and feedback** on Amazon so that it will help other people in deciding to purchase my books. I'll be very thankful to you.

If you want to write any personal note, feel free to send email at sachin@sachinsachdev.com

I respond to all the emails I receive.

Thank you
Sachin Sachdeva
Author and Illustrator

Color Testing Page

Color Testing Page

Manufactured by Amazon.ca
Bolton, ON